Dedication

Moaz Safi Yousef al-Kasasbeh
May 29, 1988–January 3, 2015

Also by Yatir Nitzany

Conversational Portuguese Quick and Easy

....

Conversational Spanish Quick and Easy

....

Conversational Italian Quick and Easy

....

Conversational French Quick and Easy

....

Conversational German Quick and Easy

....

Conversational Russian Quick and Easy

....

Conversational Polish Quick and Easy

....

Conversational Hebrew Quick and Easy

....

Conversational Yiddish Quick and Easy

....

Conversational Arabic Quick and Easy
Classical Arabic

....

Conversational Arabic Quick and Easy
Palestinian Dialect

....

Conversational Arabic Quick and Easy
Egyptian Dialect

....

Conversational Arabic Quick and Easy
Jordanian Dialect

....

Conversational Arabic Quick and Easy
Emirati Dialect

....

Conversational Arabic Quick and Easy
Iraqi Arabic

Conversational
Arabic Quick
and Easy

YEMENI DIALECT

YATIR NITZANY

Foreword

About Myself

For many years I struggled to learn Spanish, and I still knew no more than about twenty words. Consequently, I was extremely frustrated. One day I stumbled upon this method as I was playing around with word combinations. Suddenly, I came to the realization that every language has a certain core group of words that are most commonly used and, simply by learning them, one could gain the ability to engage in quick and easy conversational Spanish.

I discovered which words those were, and I narrowed them down to three hundred and fifty that, once memorized, one could connect and create one's own sentences. The variations were and are infinite! By using this incredibly simple technique, I could converse at a proficient level and speak Spanish. Within a week, I astonished my Spanish-speaking friends with my newfound ability. The next semester I registered at my university for a Spanish language course, and I applied the same principles I had learned in that class (grammar, additional vocabulary, future and past tense, etc.) to those three hundred and fifty words I already had memorized, and immediately I felt as if I had grown wings and learned how to fly.

At the end of the semester, we took a class trip to San José, Costa Rica. I was like a fish in water, while the rest of my classmates were floundering and still struggling to converse. Throughout the following months, I again applied the same principle to other languages—French, Portuguese, Italian, and Arabic, all of which I now speak proficiently, thanks to this very simple technique.

This method is by far the fastest way to master quick and easy conversational language skills. There is no other technique that compares to my concept. It is effective, it worked for me, and it will work for you. Be consistent with my program, and you too will succeed the way I and many, many others have.

Contents

Introduction to the Program. 8

Introduction to the Yemeni Dialect. 11

Memorization Made Easy 13

Arabic Pronunciation 14

Note to the Reader 15

The Program 17

Useful Vocabulary 40

Conclusion 42

INTRODUCTION TO
THE PROGRAM

People often dream about learning a foreign language, but usually they never do it. Some feel that they just won't be able to do it while others believe that they don't have the time. Whatever your reason is, it's time to set that aside. With my new method, you will have enough time, and you will not fail. You will actually learn how to speak the fundamentals of the language—fluently in as little as a few days. Of course, you won't speak perfect Yemeni dialect at first, but you will certainly gain significant proficiency. For example, if you travel to Yemen you will almost effortlessly be able engage in basic conversational communication with the locals in the present tense and you will no longer be intimidated by culture shock. It's time to relax. Learning a language is a valuable skill that connects people of multiple cultures around the world—and you now have the tools to join them.

How does my method work? I have taken twenty-seven of the most commonly used languages in the world and distilled from them the three hundred and fifty most frequently used words in any language. This process took three years of observation and research, and during that time, I determined which words I felt were most important for this method of basic conversational communication. In that time, I chose these words in such a way that they were structurally interrelated and that, when combined, form sentences. Thus, once you succeed in memorizing these words, you will be able to combine these words and form your own sentences. The words are spread over twenty pages. The words will also combine easily in sentences, for example, enabling you to ask simple questions, make basic statements, and obtain a rudimentary understanding of others' communications. I have also created Memorization Made Easy techniques for this program in order to help with the memorization of the vocabulary. Please see Reading and Pronunciation of Arabic accents in order to gain proficiency in the reading and pronunciation of the Arabic language prior to starting this program.

My book is mainly intended for basic present tense vocal communication, meaning anyone can easily use it to "get by" linguistically while visiting a foreign country without learning the entire language. With practice, you will be 100 percent understandable to native speakers, which is your aim. One disclaimer: this is not a grammar book, though it does address minute and essential grammar rules. Therefore, understanding complex sentences with obscure words in Arabic is beyond the scope of this book.

People who have tried this method have been successful, and by the time you finish this book, you will understand and be understood in basic conversational Arabic. This is the best basis to learn not only the Arabic language but any language. This is an entirely revolutionary, no-fail concept, and your ability to combine the pieces of the "language puzzle" together will come with great ease, especially if you use this program prior to beginning an Arabic class.

THE YEMENI DIALECT

The official language of Yemen, for the estimated twenty-seven million people living there, is Modern Standard Arabic, but Yemeni Arabic, which is a cluster of varieties spoken in the country and in southwestern Saudi Arabia, Somalia, and Djibouti, is unofficially used for daily communications. There are an estimated fifteen million people that use Yemeni Arabic as their primary language.

The dialect cluster is roughly divided into three main groups, each with its own distinctive vocabulary and phonology. The most important ones of these are San'ani, Ta'izzi-Adeni (also called South Yemeni Arabic or Djibouti Arabic), and Hadhrami. The dialects correspond to the three major geographical zones of the country. That is, San'ani corresponds to the regions of the capital San'a; Ta'izzi-Adeni to the regions of Aden, the former capital of South Yemen; and Hadhrami to the regions in the inner parts of the country. The Tihami dialect is also considered important and is similar to the majority of Yemeni dialects.

The dialects tend to have many features from Classical Arabic (used in Umayyad and Abbasid literary texts, 7th to 9th century AD) not found across most of the Arabic-speaking world and the cluster is, therefore, considered to be a conservative one.

Two smaller dialects, Gulf Arabic and Egyptian Arabic, have arrived in Yemen with modern migrations. There are also non-Arabic languages indigenous to the region, which have developed from the Semitic family.

Spoken in: Yemen

MEMORIZATION MADE EASY

There is no doubt the three hundred and fifty words in my program are the required essentials in order to engage in quick and easy basic conversation in any foreign language. However, some people may experience difficulty in the memorization. For this reason, I created Memorization Made Easy. This memorization technique will make this program so simple and fun that it's unbelievable! I have spread the words over the following twenty pages. Each page contains a vocabulary table of ten to fifteen words. Below every vocabulary box, sentences are composed from the words on the page that you have just studied. This aids greatly in memorization. Once you succeed in memorizing the first page, then proceed to the second page. Upon completion of the second page, go back to the first and review. Then proceed to the third page. After memorizing the third, go back to the first and second and repeat. And so on. As you continue, begin to combine words and create your own sentences in your head. Every time you proceed to the following page, you will notice words from the previous pages will be present in those simple sentences as well, because repetition is one of the most crucial aspects in learning any foreign language. Upon completion of your twenty pages, congratulations, you have absorbed the required words and gained a basic, quick-and-easy proficiency and you should now be able to create your own sentences and say anything you wish in the Yemeni Arabic dialect. This is a crash course in conversational Arabic, and it works!

ARABIC PRONUNCIATIONS

PLEASE MASTER THE FOLLOWING PAGE IN ARABIC PRONUNCIATIONS PRIOR TO STARTING THE PROGRAM

Kha. For Middle Eastern languages including Arabic, Hebrew, Farsi, Pashto, Urdu, Hindi, etc., and also German, to properly pronounce the kh or ch is essential, for example, *Khaled* (a Muslim name) or *Chanukah* (a Jewish holiday) or *Nacht* ("night" in German). The best way to describe kh or ch is to say "ka" or "ha" while at the same time putting your tongue at the back of your throat and blowing air. It's pronounced similarly to the sound that you make when clearing your throat. Please remember this whenever you come across any word containing a kh in this program.

Ghayin. The Arabic gh is equivalent to the "g" in English, but its pronunciation more closely resembles the French "r," rather than "g." Pronounce it at the back of your throat. The sound is equivalent to what you would make when gargling water. Gha is pronounced more as "rha," rather than as "ga." *Ghada* is pronounced as "rhada." In this program, the symbol for *ghayin* is gh, so keep your eyes peeled.

Aayin is pronounced as a'a, pronounced deep at the back of your throat. Rather similar to the sound one would make when gagging. In the program, the symbol for *aayin* is a'a, u'u, o'o, or i'i.

Ha is pronounced as "ha." Pronunciation takes place deep at the back of your throat, and for correct pronunciation, one must constrict the back of the throat and exhale air while simultaneously saying "ha." In the program, this strong h ("ha") is emphasized whenever *ha, ah, hi, he,* or *hu* is encountered.

NOTE TO THE READER

The purpose of this book is merely to enable you to communicate in the Yemeni Arabic dialect. In the program itself (pages 17-38) you may notice that the composition of some of those sentences might sound rather clumsy. This is intentional. These sentences were formulated in a specific way to serve two purposes: to facilitate the easy memorization of the vocabulary and to teach you how to combine the words in order to form your own sentences for quick and easy communication, rather than making complete literal sense in the English language. So keep in mind that this is not a phrase book!

As the title suggests, the sole purpose of this program is for conversational use only. It is based on the mirror translation technique. These sentences, as well as the translations are not incorrect, just a little clumsy. Latin languages, Semitic languages, and Anglo-Germanic languages, as well as a few others, are compatible with the mirror translation technique.

Many users say that this method surpasses any other known language learning technique that is currently out there on the market. Just stick with the program and you will achieve wonders!

Again, I wish to stress this program is by no means, shape, or form a phrase book! The sole purpose of this book is to give you a fundamental platform to enable you to connect certain words to become conversational. Please also read the "Introduction" and the "About Me" section prior to commencing the program.

In order to succeed with my method, please start on the very first page of the program and fully master one page at a time prior to proceeding to the next. Otherwise, you will overwhelm yourself and fail. Please do not skip pages, nor start from the middle of the book.

It is a myth that certain people are born with the talent to learn a language, and this book disproves that myth. With this method, anyone can learn a foreign language as long as he or she follows these explicit directions:

* Memorize the vocabulary on each page

* Follow that memorization by using a notecard to cover the words you have just memorized and test yourself.

* Then read the sentences following that are created from the vocabulary bank that you just mastered.

* Once fully memorized, give yourself the green light to proceed to the next page.

Again, if you proceed to the following page without mastering the previous, you are guaranteed to gain nothing from this book. If you follow the prescribed steps, you will realize just how effective and simplistic this method is.

The Program

Let's Begin! "Vocabulary" (Memorize the Vocabulary)

I | I am – A'ana
With you – (M)Ma'ak /maak – (F)Meish
With him / with her – (M)Ma-eh– (F) Ma'aaha
With us – Ma'aana
For you – (M) Lk – (F) Lesh
Without him – Bdonh / men ghaerh
Without them – Bdonhom / men ghaerohm
Always - Daymn /kol marreh/ kul saa'a
Was – Kan
This, this is - Hathae
Is, it's, it is – Ho hatha / ho dhaih /hatha ho
Sometimes – Bad alahean / ahean /zart heen
Maybe – Yemkn
You / you are - (M) A'ant / (F) a'anti
Are you – A'ant / a'anti / hu ant /hu anti
Is it – (M) ho hatha – (F) hee hathah
Today – Alyoum
Better – Ahsan
He / he is - Ho
She / she is - Hee
From - Men
From where – Men aynh

This is for you
Hatha lk / lesh
I am from Yemen
A'ana Men al-yamn
Are you from Sana'a?
A'ant / a'anti men san'aa'?
I am with you
A'ana ma'ak / Me-ish
Sometimes you are with us at the mall
Bad alahean a'ant ma'ana fe almool
I am always with her
A'ana daymn Ma'aaha
Are you without them today?
A'ant Bdonhom alyoum?
Sometimes I am with him
Bad alahean a'ana ma-eh

*In Arabic with the question "is it?", the "it" can pertain to either a masculine or feminine noun. However, whenever pertaining to a masculine or feminine noun, it will become *ho* (m) / *hee* (f). For example, when referring to a feminine noun such as *sayaara* (the car), "is it (the car in question) here?" / *Hal hee hana?* When referring to a masculine noun such as *kaleb* (a dog), "is it (the dog in question) on the table?" / *Hal ho fawq elmasah?*

I was - Kont
To be - (M) yoga'a / (F) toga'ay
The - Al
Same – (M) Nafseh /sa'aeh (F) Nafseha/sa'aeha
Good – Haly / saber / eis / jaid / jeed /tamam
Here - Hana
Very / much – Gawy, khayrat
And - Wa
Between – Bayn
Now – Thalheen/a'alaan
Later / after / afterwards – Ba'ada /ba'ad
If – Law / etha
Yes – Aywah /na'am
To – La /ala seb
Tomorrow – Ghodoah / bokrh / bokreh
You - (M) a'ant (F) a'anti
Also / too / as well – Walkol

If it's between now and later
Law ho been thalheen wa ba'ada / Law Ayouga'a been thalheen wa ba'ada
It's better tomorrow
Alahsan ghodoah
This is good as well
Hatha haly / saber /tamam walkol
To be the same person
Ala seb toga'a nafs alshakhs
Yes, you are very good
Aywah, a'ant haly gawy
I was here with them
A'ana kont hana ma'aahom
You and I
A'ant wa ana
The same day
Nafs alyaoum

*In Yemini dialect the word "good" depends on your reference. For example, the "good" in "good morning" is "khair" if you said "I am good" is "a'ana bekhair" when you say "this is a good work" it's "saber" or "tamam", however "haly" means "sweet".

Me - A'ana
Ok – Tamam / aies / jaid
Even if - Walw
No – Ma'a /mashi /laa
Worse – Shoa'ah
Where – Wayn / aynah
Everything – Kol she / alkull
Somewhere – Boga'ah /makaan
What – Mahoo/Aysho
Almost – Tagreebn / sa'a
There – Haanaak /honk ka

Afterwards is worse
Men ba'ada ashoa'a /akhass
Even if I go now
Hataa Walw aseer thalheen /hataa walw sert thalheen
Where is everything?
Wayn/aino kol she /aino kol she/aina alkull
Maybe somewhere
Yemken fe boga'ah katha wella katha /Yemken makan hana wella hanak
What? I am almost there
Aysh? /Mahoo? A'ana tagreebn hanak
Where are you?
(M) Wayn ant? / A'ain ant? / (F) wayn anti? A'ain anti?
Where is the airport?
Wayn/ain almatar?

Fe boga'ah /fe ay boga'ah literally means "in a place."

*In Yemeni Arabic, the pronoun "me" has several definitions. In relation to verbs, it's *(le)*. *(Le)* refers to any verb that relates to the action of doing something to someone or for someone.
For example, "tell me," "tell (to) me" / *(M) gowlle*
(ani) just means "me": "love me" / *(yehbani)*
Other variations *(ya, ny, e, y):*
* "on me" /*alya*, "in me" / *feny*
* "to me" / *le*, "with me" /*meiy*
The same rule applies for "him" and "her"—both become suffixes: *–o* and *–a*. Basically all verbs pertinent to males end with *(o)* and all pertinent to female end with *(ee)*.
* "love her" / *yehbaha*, "love him" / *tehbah*
* "love them" / *yehbhom*, "love us" / *yehbana*
Any verb that relates to doing someone to someone, for someone put *l:*
* "tell her" / *gollaha*, "tell him" / *gollah*
* "tell them" / *gollohm*, "tell us" / *gollana*
Adding you as a suffix in Arabic is *(ak)* or *(lak),* female *(esh)*, or *(lek)*
* "love you" / (M) *ahebak* / (F) *ahbesh*, "tell you" / *(M) agollak* / (F) *agollek*

House - Bait
In / at – Fe /end
Car - Sayarah
Already – Thalheen /a'alaan /hadhi asa'a
Good morning – Sabah alkhaeer
How are you? – Kaeef ant / anti
Where are you from? – (M) Men ain ant? / (F) men ain anti?
Today - Alyaoum
Hello - Salam
What is your name? – (M) Besmak / (F) besmesh
How old are you? - (M) Kam omrak? / (F) kam omresh?
Son – Wald /ibn /welaid
Daughter – Bent / Binayeh
To have – (M) Yemlaak (F) temlaak
Doesn't – Mabesh
Hard – Sa'ab
Still – **(M)** Adoo /aad-hoo / **(F)** adey /aad-hee
Then (or "so") – Ya'any /woo ba'ada /yeji

She doesn't have a car, so maybe she is still at the house?
Mabesh ma'aaha sayarah, ya'any yemken adye /aad-hee fe albeit?
Mabesh ma'aaha sayarah, yeji we-adaha fe albeit?

I am in the car already with your son and daughter
A'ana fe alsayarah a'alaan ma'aa ibnak we bentak
qadnaa dakhel alsayarah a'alaan ma'aa ibnak we bentak
qadnaa dakhel alsayarah thalheen ma'aa ibnak we bentak

Good morning, how are you today?
Sabah alkhaeer, kaeef ant alyaoum?

Hello, what is your name?
Salam, besmak?

How old are you?
Kam omrak?

This is very hard, but it's not impossible
Hatha sa'ab qaway, lakn masho mostaheel /laikn masho mostaheel

Then where are you from?
Ya'any men ayn ant? We ba'ada menin ant?

*In Yemeni Arabic, the verb "to have" translates into the phrase "with me," "with you," "with him," "with her," "with them," and "with us."

"I have" is, *meie* which also means "with me." "You have" is *maak* or *ma'ak* for masculine and *meish* for feminine, and also means "with you." "They have" is *maahom*, which also means "with them," and "We have" is *maana* which also means "with us."

"He has" is *mee-ih* and "she has" is *ma'aaha,* which also mean "with him" / "with her."

*When using negations in regards to the verb "have," we use *mabesh*. "I don't have" /*mabesh maa'ya, me-ei* / *mei-ya* "she doesn't have"/ *mabesh ma'aaha*, "he doesn't have" / *mabesh me-eh*, "You don't have" / *mabesh ma'ak*, etc.

*In Arabic, possessive pronouns become suffixes to the noun. For example, in the translation for "your," *ak* is the masculine form, and *ek* is the feminine form.

-"your book" / *ketabak* (m.), *ketabesh* (f.)/ "your house" / *baeetak* (m.), *baeetesh* (f.)

Thank you - Shokrn lak /ash-kurk /ess-lm

For – La

Anything - Aye shee

That / That is – (M) Hathak /Hathk-ka / (F) hathek

Time - Wagt/ sa'ah / marrah

But - Laken / lai-ken

No / not – Ma'a /maa'a/mashi/mash-sho

I am not - Msh ana /manash / msh-sho a'ana

Away - Be-eid

Late – Mit-a'akher /shaaraq

Similar – Me-shabeh / shabah /sa'a /nafs

Another/ other – Althany

Side – Jehah / jamb

Until – Lawma /heta /la-end

Yesterday - Ams

Without us – Bdonana

Since - Men/men ayheen/men lama

Day - Yaoum

Before – Gabl

Thanks for everything
Shokrn ala kol shee

I am not here, I am away
Mosh ana hana, ana ba'aeed
Maba –had ana hana, a'ana be-ied
Mshna hana, a'ana be-ied

That is a similar house
Hatha baeet moshabeh
Hatha baeet sa'a-eh.
Hatha baeet me-shabeh leh.

I am from the other side
Ana men aljehah althanyah
A'ana men aljehah almeqablah

But I was here until late yesterday
Laken ana kont ams hana la mota'aker
Lai-ken a'ana kont hana la waqt met-a'akher ams

I am not at the other house
Mosh ana fe albeet althany
Mshana fe albeet althany
Manash fe albeet althany

---

*In Yemeni Arabic, there are three definitions for time:
- "time" / *wagt* refers to "era", "moment period," "duration of time."
- "time(s)"/ *marrah(t)* / *karrah(t)* refers to "occasion" or "frequency."
- "time" / *sa'ah* references "hour," "what time is it?"

*In the Arabic language, as well as in other Semitic languages, the article "a" doesn't exist. "She doesn't have a car" / *mabesh ma'aaha sayarah.*
*In Yemeni Arabic, with negations such as "no," "not," "doesn't," "can't," and "don't," use either *ma'a, mosh, mash, mabesh,* or *la. La* is used to indicate cases such as "are you here" – *ant hena* – and you then reply "no," *la. Mosh* or *mash* is used to indicate cases of "not," "doesn't," or "don't," for example: "I am not here" is *mosh ana hena.* In some instances, both cases of *la* and *mosh* may be used, for example; "no I am not here" is *la, mosh ana hena.* However, *mabesh* or *ma'a /ma'ah* are usually used to negate cases of verbs.
This isn't a phrase book! The purpose of this book is solely to provide you with the tools to create your own sentences!

I say / I am saying - Aqol / baenaqol

What time is it? - Kam alsa'ah? Kam qadee? Kam qada alasa'ah

I want – A'ashty

Without you – (M) Bdonak / (F) bdonesh

Everywhere /wherever – Kol boqa'ah / aye boqa'ah/kol makan /ain ma kan

I go - Aseer

With- Ma'aa

My – E /haqi / ta-baee

Cousin (paternal) - (M) Ibn amy / (F) bent amy /(P)(M) eal amy / (P)(F) banat amy

Cousin (maternal) - (M) Ibn khaly / (F) bent khaly /(P)(M) eal khaly / (P)(F) banat khaly

I need – Ahtaj/ashty

Right now – Thalheen/a'alaan/hathi alsa'a

Night – Alashy

To see – Yebser /yesta-dhi

Light - Daw

Outside - Kharej

Without - Bdon

Happy – Fareh/murtah / meftehen

I see / I am seeing – Benabser/ benasta-dhi

I want to see this today
A'ashty abser hatha alyaoum

I am with you everywhere
A'a na ma'ak fe kol boqa'ah / A'ana ma'ak fe kol makan

I am happy without my cousins here
A'a na fareh/mortah bdon ibn amy hana

I need to be there at night
A'ashty akon hanak alashy

I see light outside
Benabser daw kharej

What time is it right now?
Kam alsa'ah thalheen/a'alan

---

*"Mine" / (*haqy*) is also a possessive pronoun. *E* means "my" but also becomes a suffix to a noun. Nouns ending in a vowel end with *–teh*. Nouns ending with a consonant end with *–eh*. For example:

"cousin" / *ibn alam*/ "my cousin "/ *ibn amy*, "cup" / *galas*/ "my cup" / *galasy*

For second and third person masculine noun, *ibn* / "son", male (S) *ak*, (P) *akom*, and female (S) *ek*, (P) *ken*. "His" – *ah*. / "hers" – *ha*, noun endings will be *o* (for male) and *a* (for female).

"your son" / *ibnak* (m.) *ibnesh* (f.), "your (plural) son" /*ealkom* (m.), *ealaken* (f.), "his son" / *ibnh*, "her son" /*ibnaha*, "our son"/*ibnana'a*, "their son"/*ealohom* (m.), *ealehen* (f.)

For second and third person feminine noun: "car" / *sayarah*

"your car" / *sayaratk*, "your (plural) car" / *sayartkom*, "his car" / *sayarath*, "her car" / *sayartha*, "our car" / *sayartna*, "their car" / *sayarthom*

Place – Makan / boqa'ah
Easy - Sahal
To find – Yelqa /yehasel / yelfa
To look for / to search – Yedowr /yebhath
Near / Close – Jamb/qareeb
To wait - Yera'aie /yentadher
To sell - (M) Yebiea'a / (F) tebiea'a
To do - Yefa'al
To use - Yestakhdem
To know – Yedra'a / yeeref
To decide – Yeaqarar /yekhtar
Between - Bayn
Both – Jama'ah/ma'a ba'ad
To – La / end
In order to – Eno /ala-shan /ala seb

This place it's easy to find
Hatha almakan /hathaeh alboqa'ah sahal eno nelqah/nelqaha
I want to look for this next to the car
A'ashty adowr hatha jamb alsayarah
I am saying to wait until tomorrow
A'a na ben aqol eno nera'ay/nen tadher la ghodwah
This table is easy to sell (to be sold)
Hathah almasah sahal eno nebyaha
I want to use this
A'ashty a'astakhdem hatha
I need to know where (location) is the house
A'ashty adra'a ayno makan/aene boqa'at albaeet
I want to decide between both places
A'ashty aqaraer bayn alethneen alamaken / althentain albooqa'a

---

*In Yemeni Arabic, to indicate "to," either la or *eno* or *ashan* may be used. *La* is placed preceding a noun. *Eno* is used preceding a verb, while *alashan* /*ala-sebb* is mostly used to indicate "in order to." In certain instances, both *ashan* and *la* may be used, for example: "There isn't enough time to go to Taiz today" / *mabesh waqt kafy alashan* /*ala-sebb aseer la ta'iz alyaoum.*

Because - La'ano /le-ann
To buy – Yeshtree
They - Hom
Them / their – Hom / hom
Bottle – Zejajeh/qarooreh
Book - Ketab
Mine - Haqy
To understand – Yefham/yedrek /yedh-hr leh
Problem / Problems - Moshkelah /mashakel
I do / I am doing - Afa'al / ben afa'al
Of – Haq - However in some contexts it is useless
To look – Yebser
Myself – Nafsy
Enough – Yekfee/ kefaayeh
Food / water – Akl /me-a'a
Each/ every/ entire/ all – Kol
Hotel - Fondoq

I like this hotel because I want to look at the beach
Ajabni hatha alfodoq la'ano ashtee abser alshata'a
I want to buy a bottle of water
A'ashty a'ashtaree qarrowrah maa'a/mae
I do this every day
Ben afa'al hatha kol yaoum
Both of them have enough food
Alethnaeen jam'ah /hola alethneen ma'ahom keyfaithum akl
That is the book, and that book is mine
Hathak ho alketab, wa hathak alketab ho haqy
I need to understand the problem
Ahtaj / a'ashty afham almoshkelah
I see the view of the city from the hotel
Ben Abser almandar haq almadenah men alfondoq
I do my homework today
Ben afa'al haqy alwajeb alyoum
My entire life (*all my life*)
Hayati kolaha (kol hayati)

*"At the" the "at" is often useless, however sometimes "at" translates into *fe*.

*"Both of them" is *alethnaeen jama'ah*.

I like - Yeajebni
There is / There are – Beh hana / beh nanak
Family / Parents - Ayelah / omi wa abi/ alwaldain /alwaled wa alwaldah
Why – Laysh/ lelmeh
To say – Yeqol
Something – Hajah /shee
To go – (M) Yiseer / (F) tiseer
Ready – Jahez
Soon - Qareeb/ thalheen/ a'alaan
To work – (M) Yishtagel / (F) tishtagel
Who – Mn / mn hoo
To know - Yearef/ yedra'a
That (conjunction) - Alathy /ally / eno (m)/ enaha (f)

I like to be at my house with my parents
Yajebni akon fe albaeet maa'a omi wa abi / alwaled wa alwaldeh
I want to know why I need to say something important
Ashte a'aref laysh ahtaj eno aqol hajah mehemah
I am there with him
A'a na hanak maa'ah /a'ana hanak ka mea'ah
I am busy, but I need to be ready soon
A'a na mashgol, lakn / laiken ahtaj akon jahez thalheen / a'alaan
I like to go to work
Yajebni asser alamal / la alamal
'Who is there?
Mano hanak
I want to know if they are here, because I want to go outside
A'ashty a'aref/ adra'a etha hom hana, la'ano / la'any ashti akhorj
There are seven dolls
Beh hanak saba'a arays
I need to know that it is a good idea
A'ashty a'aref enaha fekrah haleah/jaiedah /iesah

*In the last sentence, we use "that" as a conjunction (*eno/enaha*) and a demonstrative pronoun (M) *hatha* / (F) *hathae*.

How much /how many – Km
To bring – Yidee
To take – Yeshll / yebez
With me – Mea'ae /meeyaa
Instead – Badal/ ghaer
Only – Bas / mabesh ghair / faqt
When – Ayheen
Or – Aw / wella
I can / Can I – A'aqder / a'aqder? /A'aster
Were – Kano
Without me - Bdony
Fast – Bisra'ah/sarea'a
Slow – Batei / dala
Cold – Bard/saamett
Inside - Dakhel
To eat – Yakol
Hot – Hamy
To Drive – Yesouq

How much money do I need to bring with me?
Kam zaltt ahtaj adee maa'ay?
Instead of this cake, I want that cake
Badal hatheh alkekah, a'ashty hathek /hathek ka alkekah
Only when you can
Bas/ faqt lawma teqder
They were without me yesterday
Hom kano bdony ams
Do I need to drive the car fast or slow?
Ahtej asouq alsayarah besor'ah aw/ wella bebota'a /dala
It is cold inside the library
Bard dakhel almaktabah
Yes, I like to eat this hot for my lunch
Aywah, a'ashty akol hatha hamy la haqy alghada'a
I can work today
A'aqder a'ashtegel alyaoum

*"Were" is *kano*, "they were" is also *kano*, but for "we were" is *kona*.

*"I can" and "can I?" could either be *aqder*. "You can" or "can you?" is *teqder?*

26

To answer (the phone) - Yejaweb
To fly - Yeteer
Time / Times – Marrah / marrat /waqt / awqat / karreh /karrat
To travel – Yesafer
To learn - (M) Yeta'alam /yeqrae/ yedres (F) teta'alam /teqra'a /tesres
How - Kaeef
To swim - (M) Yesbah / (F) tesbah /yetsabbah / tetssabah
To practice – Yemares/yetmarn / yetraiadh
To play – Yela'ab
To leave – Yeseer /yerehleh (for going) / yekhaly / yefalet (for things)
Many /much /a lot - Khayrat
I go to – Sert la
First – Awal
World - 'Ala'alam / aldeneea

I want to answer many questions
A'ashty ajaweb asa'aelah khayrat
I must fly to Dubai today
Dharory asafer la Dubai alyaoum
I need to learn how to swim at the pool
A'ashty ata'alam kaeef asbah/attsabah fe hawd alsebaha'a
I want to learn to play better tennis
A'ashty ata'alam alab altennis ahsan
I want to leave this here for you when I go to travel the world
A'ashty akhaly hatha hana lak lawma aseer asafer la alalam
Since the first time
Men awal marreh
The children are yours
Hathawla eialak /hawla eialak

* In Yemeni Arabic, "to leave (something)" is *yefalet / yekhaley* "To leave (a place)" is *yerehleh/ yeghader*. For example, "please leave this place" *law samaht qom rehlak* so "*yerehleh*" is coming from "*rehlaak a'alaan*" means "leave now").

* In Yemeni Arabic, there are three definitions for time:
- "time" / *waqt* refers to "era", "moment period," "duration of time."
- "time(s)"/ *marra(t)* / *karra(t)* refers to "occasion" or "frequency."
- "time" / *sa'ah* references "hour," "what time is it?"

* In Yemeni Arabic *net'allam* is used to signify the verb "to learn," however for masculine cases we use *yeta'alam* and for feminine case we use *teta'alam*.

*With the knowledge you've gained so far, now try to create your own sentences!

Nobody / anyone – Mahad / aywahed

Against – Dhed

Us – Lana

To visit - Yezor / yezawer

Mom / Mother – Omi / alwaledeh

To give – Yedi

Which – Alathy /ally

To meet - Yeqabel

Someone – Ahad

Just – Bas /mabesh ghair / faqt

To walk - Yekhta'a

Around – Haol /dar ma dar

Towards – Laend / sala

Than - Men

Nothing – Mabesh /wala-she

Something is better than nothing
Hajah ahsan men / mabesh / Shee ahsen men wala-shee

I am against him
A'a na dhedeh

Is there anyone here?
Beh ahad hana?

We go to visit my family each week
Benseer nezor ayalati / osratey kol esboa'a

I need to give you something
Ahtaj adelak hajah

Do you want to go meet someone?
Teshty teseer teqabel ahad?

I was here on Wednesdays as well
A'ana kont hana alraboa'a walkol
A'ana kont hana kol raboa'a walkol

Do you do this every day?
Betfa'al hatha kol yaoum?

You need to walk around, but not towards the house
Atehtaj tekhta'a haol /dar ma dar lakn/lai-ken mosh sala / laend albait

---

*In Yemeni Arabic, when using the pronoun "you" as a direct and indirect object pronoun (the person who is actually affected by the action that is being carried out) in relation to a verb, the pronoun "you" becomes a suffix to that verb. That suffix becomes *ak* (masc.) *ek* (fem.).

- "to give" / *yedi* "to give you" /*yedilak*.
- "to tell" / *yoqol* "to tell you" / *yoqolak* (m.), *yoqolek* (f.)
- "see you" / *yebserak* "to see you" (plural) / *yebsorokom* (m.), *yebsoroken* (f.)

For third person male, add *h* and *om* for plural, for female add *ha* and *hn* for plural.

- "tell him" / *qoleh*
- "tell her" / *qoleha*
- "see them" /*ebserhom* (m.), *ebserehn* (f.)
- "see us " / *ebserona*

I have – Meie/meiya
Don't - La
Friend -(M) Saheb /**(F)** saheba
To borrow – Yesta'aeer / yetsalaaf
To look like / resemble – Yeshbah / yoqa'a sa'a
Like (preposition) **-** Methl/sa'a
Grandfather – Jad / seed
To want - Yeshty
To stay - Yejles
To continue - Yewasel
Way – Tareeq
I don't - Ma
To show - Yeowary
To prepare - Yejahez
I am not going – Ma ada

Do you want to look like Salim
Teshty toqa'a sa'a Salim?
I want to borrow this book for my grandfather
A'ashty asta'aeer hatha alketab lae jady
I want to drive and to continue on this way to my house
A'ashty asooq wa awasel ala hatha altareeq la baeety
I have a friend there, that's why I want to stay in Aden
Meie sahib hanak, lehatha a'ashty ajles fe 'adan
I am not going to see anyone here
Ma adabsersh ahwahed hana
I need to show you how to prepare breakfast
A'ashty awaryk kaeef nejahez saboh
Why don't you have the book?
Laysh mabesh maa'ak alketab?
That is incorrect, I don't need the car today
Hathak /hathak ka mosh sah, ana ma ahtajsh alsayarah alyaoum

To remember - Yetthakar
Your - (M) Ak / **(F)**esh
Number - Raqam
Hour – Sa'ah
Dark / darkness – Dholmy
About / on the – Alashan /ala seb (regarding) / ala (on top of something)
Grandmother - Jaddah
Minute / minutes – Daqeqah /daqaeq
More - Akthar
To think – Yefaker
To do – Yefa'al
To come – Yejee
To hear – Yesma'a
Last – Akher

You need to remember my number
'Atehtaj eno/inak tetthakar raqmy
This is the last hour of darkness
Hathah akher sa'ah dhulmee
I want to come and to hear my grandmother speak Yemeni Arabic
A'ashty ajee wa asma'a jadaty betetkalam/ betethaka yemeni
I need to think more about this, and what to do
Ahtaj afaker akthar an hatha, wa aysh afa'al
From here to there, it's only five minutes
Men hana la hanak, he bas khams daqaeq
The school on the mountain
Almadrash fawq aljabal

*In Yemeni Arabic *alashan / ala seb* is used to signify "about/regarding." However to indicate cases of "on top of something, on top of a place" we use *ala*, for example, *ala aljabal* "on the mountain" is a place, so in this case, we will use *ala*.

To leave - Yefallet (to leave something) / yerehleh (to leave somewhere)
Again – Marrah thanyah
Yemen – Al-yaman
To take - Yakhoth/ yeshell /yebez
To try - Yehawel
To rent – Yesta'ajer
Without her - Bdonaha
We are – Ehna
To turn off – Yetafee /yeghaleq
To ask – Yesa'al
To stop - Yewaqef
Permission - Ethn

He needs to leave and rent a house at the beach
Yehtaj yeseer wa yesta'ajer bait ala alshatea'a/ alsahel
I want to take the test without her
A'ashty akhoth alemtahan bdonaha
We are here a long time
Qd lana waqt hana / ehna hana men fatrah tawelah (*fatra* means "a while")
I need to turn off the lights early tonight
A'ashty atafee aldhaw alylah badri
We want to stop here
Neshty newaqef hana
We are from Al-hudaydah
Ehna men al-hedaydah
The same building
Nafs albenayah
I want to ask permission to leave
A'ashty asta'athen ala seb / alashaan aseer
I want to sleep
A'ashty anam /arqod

*In Yemeni Arabic, "to stop" is *yewaqef*, "to cease" is also *khalas*. For example, if someone is bothering you, you tell them, "Stop!" / *khalas!*
*In Yemeni Arabic, *yeshell* and *yebez* are used to signify the verb "to take". However, they are used when referring to the action of taking physical items. For example, "take this bag with you" in Sanaani dialect will be *shell hatha alkees ma'ak*.

To open - Yeftah
A bit, a little, a little bit - Qaleel / shuaiah
To pay – Yedfa'a / yehaseb
Once again – Marrah thanyah
There isn't/ there aren't – Mabesh hanak
Sister - Okht
To hope – Yea'amel / Yetmanna
To live - Yeaeesh
Nice to meet you – Forsah sa'aeedah
Name - Alesm
Last name – Allaqab
To return – Yeraja'a
Sad - Za'ael / hazeen
United States - Amreeca
Door - Baab

I need to open the door for my sister
A'ashty aftah albab la okhty
I need to buy something
A'ashty ashtray hajah
I want to meet your sisters
A'ashty aqabel khawatak
Nice to meet you, what is your name and your last name
Forsah sa'aeedah, Me esmk / besmak? Mahoo laqabak? Aisho laqabak?
To hope for a little better
Yetmana ahsan shuaiah
I want to return from the United States and to live in Qatar without problems
A'ashty arja'a men amreeca wa aeesh fe Qatar bdon mashakel
Why are you sad right now?
Laysh ant za'ael/hazeen dhalheen?
There aren't people here
Mabsh nas hana
There isn't enough time to go to Taiz today
Mabesh waqt kafy ashan aseer la ta'iz alyaoum

*In Yemeni Arabic, regarding the verb "to meet," there are two separate cases to define this verb: *yeqabel* and *yeta'raf*, depending of the context. To meet for business is *yeqabel*. To meet for getting acquainted is *yeta'raf*. In the sentence, "Do you want to go meet someone?" (the sister, getting acquainted with her), it's *yeta'raf*.

*This *isn't* a phrase book! The purpose of this book is *solely* to provide you with the tools to create *your own* sentences

To happen – Yehsal /yoqa'a
To order – Yoa'amr /yewajjeh
To drink - Yeshrab
Excuse me - **(M)** Law samaht /afwn **(F)** law samahti
Child - (M)Ibn /jahel / Wald (F)jaheleh/ ibnah /*benaeyeh*
Woman - Marah
To begin / to start – Yebda'a
To finish - Yekammel/ yekhaless
To help – Yesa'aed / ye-a'awin
To smoke - Yeshaqer
To love - Yeheb / yehnaaj/ yeishq
To talk / to speak – Yet-haka/ yetkallam

This must happen today
Hatha lazem/ dharoori yoqa'a/yehsl alyaoum
Excuse me, my child is here as well
Law samaht, waladi/ ibny hana walkol
I love you
(M)Ahebak /(F) Ahebesh
I see you
Baen abserak / ben astadheek
I need you at my side
Ahtatjak jamby
I need to begin soon to be able to finish at 3 o'clock in the afternoon
A'ashty abda'a badri alashaan /ala seb aqder akamel alsa'ah 3 ba'ad aldhor
I need help
Ahtaj mesa'adah
I don't want to smoke once again
Ma a'ashtysh /ma ad ashteesh / mshteesh ashqer marrah thanyah
I want to learn how to speak Arabic
A'a shty ata'alm kaeef at-haaka / atkalam Arabi

*In Yemeni Arabic to signify "love" we can either use *ahanj* or *aheb* or *a'ashaj*
*In Yemeni dialect there are several variations for the definition of "child".
For example, "he is just a kid" - *hoo ilaa jahel* / "who is the mother of this child?"
- *men he amm hatha alwald/ aljahel?* / "he is the son of who?" - "*ibn men ho hathaa alwald.*

To read - Yeqra **/** yedress (*yedress* is used especially for reading quran)
To write- Yektob
To teach - Yedarres/ yeqaree
To close -Yeghaleg/ yeqaffel
To choose - Yekhtar/ yenaqi
To prefer - Yefadhel
To put - Yetrah
Less - Aqll
Sun - Shams
Month - Shahr
I talk – At-haaka / Tehakeet (in the past)
Exact - Baldhabd /tamamn

I need this book to learn how to read and write in Arabic because I want to teach in Egypt
Ahtaj hatha alketab ala seb ata'alam kaeef aqra wa aktob balarabi la'ano/le-a'any a'ashty adrress fe masr
I want to close the door of the house
A'ashty aghaleg bab albaeet/ albab hq albaeet
I prefer to put the gift here
A'ana afadhel eno netrah alhadyah hana
I want to pay less than you for the dinner
A'ashty adfa'a /ahaseb aqal menak la alasha'a/hq alasha'a
I speak with the boy and the girl in French
Hen at-haka ma'a alwald wa albent balfaransi /ben ahaka alwald wa albent balfaransi.
There is sun outside today
Beh shams kharej alyoum
Is it possible to know the exact date?
Momken aref altarekh baldhabd?

*"For the" is *la*.

*"In" is *bal*.

With the knowledge you've gained so far, now try to create your own sentences!

To exchange (money**)** – Yesruf/ Yebaddel
To call – Yetasel
Brother – Akh
Dad – Abb / waled
To sit – Yejles
Together - Jama'ah /ma'aa ba'adh
To change – Yeghaeer /yebaddel
Of course - Akeed
Welcome - Ahlan
During – Towl / waqt ma/ sa'at ma /khilal
Years - (**S**) Sanah / (**P**) seneen
Sky - Sama
Up – Fawq/ talei
Down - Taht / nazel
Sorry - Asef
To follow – (M)Yeseer bada'aeh / yelhaaq / yetba'a / (F)badaha
To the – La end
Big - Kabeer
New - Jadeed
Never / ever - Abadn / hata law
Him / her - Ah / ha

I don't want to exchange this money at the bank
Mashtysh abadel / asruf hatheh alzalatt fe albank
I want to call my brother and my dad today
A'ashty atasel la akhi wa abi alyaoum
Of course I can come to the theater, and I want to sit together with you and with your sister
Akeed aqder ajee la almasrah, wa a'ashty ajles ma'ak ant wo aukhtk jamma'a
I need to go down to see your new house
A'ashty anzel ala seb abser baeetak aljadeed
I can see the sky from the window
Aqder abser alsama men alttaqah
I am sorry, but he wants to follow her to the store
A'a na asef, lakn / lai ken ho yeshty yeseer badaha la albaqalah
I don't ever want to see you again
A'a na mashtysh hata abserak marrah thanea
A'ana ma ad astesh abserak marrah thaneah

*In Yemeni dialect, brother is *akh,* and dad is *abb.* However, "my dad" is *abi* and "my brother" is *akhi.* "My sister" is *okhti*, and "my mother" is *omi.*

To allow - Yesmah / yekhalee
To believe – Yesadeq
Morning – Sobh /sabbah
Except - Ma'ada / ella
To promise - Yoed
Good night - Tesbeh ala khaeer
To recognize - Yefham / yestaweb
People - Naas
To move – Yet-harak / yenqull
Far - Be-eid
Different – Mokhtalef /mash-sho sawa
Man – Rajjal / a'adami
To enter - Yedkhol
To receive – Yestalem / yestaqbel
Throughout - Fe kol makan / fe kol boqa'a
Good evening – Masa'a alkhaeer
Left / right - Yasar / yameen

I need to allow him to go with us, he is a different man now
A'ashty asmahleh / akhaleeh yeseer ma'ana, ala'an ho rajal mokhtalef
I believe everything except this
A'a na asadeq kolshee ma'ada/ella hatha
I promise to say good night to my parents each night
Wa'ad eni aqol tosbeho ala khaeer la omi wa abi kol laylah
The people from Jordan are very pleasant
Alnas (alathy) men alardon latefeen qawy
I need to find another hotel very quickly
Ahtaj/ A'ashty /alqaa /ahassel fondoq thany besora'ah
They need to receive a book for work
(Hom) yeshto / yehtajw (eno) yestalemo ketab lal alamal
I see the sun in the morning
Benabser alsham alsobh /fe alsabah
The house is on the right side of the street
Albaeet fe lajehah alyameen men alsharea

*For the possessive pronouns, her *ha* and him *h*, both become suffixes to the verb or noun. Concerning nouns: her house / *baeetaha,* his house / *baeeteh).* Concerning cases regarding verbs, please see footnotes on page 19.

To wish – Yetmana / yehlaam
Bad - Shoa'ah / msh-sho haly
To get - Yoqa'a
To forget - Yensa
Everybody / Everyone - Kolwahed
Although - (M) Ma'a eno / (F) ma'a enaha
To feel – Yehes / yesh-or
Great – Adheem /momtaz
Next (as in close, near) – Jamb
Next (as in next year) – Aljaeeh /(M)aljayee / ally a'a yeji (F)aljayeeah / ally a'atigi
To like – Yeshty
In front – Qudam / qubal
Person – Shakhs / aadmi
Behind – Wara / qaafa
Well – Murtah /meftehn / tamam /saber
Restaurant - Mata'am
Bathroom - Hamam
Goodbye - Ma'aslamah / fe aman ellah

I don't want to wish you anything bad
Mashtysh atmana lak ayshee shoa'ah
I must forget everybody from my past to feel well
Lazem/ Dharori ansa kolwahed men almady ala seb ahes in-ani murtah
I am next to the person behind you
A'ana / jamb alshkhs / aladmi (alathy/ally) waraq/ qafak
There is a great person in front of me
Beh shakhs adheem qudami
I say goodbye to my friends
A'ana dayeman aqool la ashabi ma'aslamah
Where is the bathroom in the restaurant?
Ayn alhamam fe almata'am
She has to get a car before the next year
Lazem / Dharori yoqa'a laha sayarah qabl alsanal aljaheeh / qabl alsanah ally a'atigi
I like the house, but it is very small
Ejabny albaeet, lakn/ lai ken ino segheer qawy

Jamb literally means "side." In Arabic, it refers to "next." *Jambi* is "besides me" and *jambak* is "besides you."

To remove / to take out – Yebead / yelghee /yeqla'a
Please - Law samaht / men fadh-luck
Beautiful - (**M**) Jameel / haly / (**F**) jameelah / halyah
To lift – Yerfa'a
Include / Including - Ma'a / bain
Belong – Makaneh/ taba'a
To hold - Yemsak/ yeshbaah / yezqaam
To check – Yetahaqaq / yeta'aked/ yefhaas
Small - Sagheer
Real - Haqeqi / asli
Fake – Kadhby / msho asli
Week – Esboo / osboo
Size - Hajm
Even though - Hata wa-law/ hata etha
Doesn't - Ma
So (as in "then") – Ya'any
So (as in "so big") - Qawy
Price - Sea'ar

She wants to remove this door please
Hiya eshty tebead / teqla'a hatha albab law samaht
This doesn't belong here, I need to check again
Hatha masho makaneh hana, ahtaj/ a'ashty atahqaq/ata'aked marrah thaneah
This week the weather was very beautiful
Hatha alesboo/ alosboo aljaw kan jameel jedn
Hatha alesboo/ alosboo aljaw kan rawa'ah
Hatha alesboo/ alosboo aljaw kan mashallah
I need to know which is the real diamond
Ahtaj/ a'ashty a'aref ayanho alalmas alhaqyqi/alasli
We need to check the size of the house
Neshty / nehtaj netahqaq/ neta'akd men hajm albaeet
I want to lift this, so you need to hold it high
A'ashty arfa'a hatha, lethalek dharoori temsakah la fawq/talie
I can pay this even though that the price is expensive including everything is this price correct?
Aqder adfa'a/ahaseb hq hatha wa-law inn hathak alser ghaly ma'aa kolshy, hatha alser qadoo alsahih?

Countries of the Middle East

Lebanon - Lobnan
Syria - Sorya
Jordan - Alardon
Saudi Arabia - Alsa'awdeah
Israel / Palestine / *West Bank* -
Israel / falsteen / aldefah
algharbeah
Bahrain - Albahreen
Yemen - Alyaman
Oman - Oman
United Arab Emirates - Alemarat
alarabeh almotahedah
Kuwait - Alkuwait
Iraq - Aleraq
Qatar - Qatar
Morocco - Almaghreb
Algeria - Aljazaer
Libya - Libya
Egypt - Masr
Tunisia - Tunis

Months

January - Yanaer
February - Febrayr
March – Mares
April - Ebreel
May - Mayo
June - Yoneo
July - Yoleo
August - Augustos
September - Setember
October - October
November - Nofember
December - December

Days of the Week

Sunday - Ahad
Monday - Ethnaeen
Tuesday - Thaloth
Wednesday – Rabowa'a
Thursday - Khames
Friday - Jomoah
Saturday - Sabt

Seasons

Spring – Rabei
Summer - Sayf
Autumn - Khareef
Winter – Sheta'a

Cardinal Directions

North - Shamal
South - Janob
East – Sharq
West – Gharb

Colors

Black - Aswad
White - Abyad
Gray - Ramady
Red - Ahmar
Blue - Azraq
Yellow - Asfar
Green - Akhtar
Orange – Bortoqaly
Purple - Banafsjy
Brown – Bony

Numbers

One - Wahed
Two - Ethnaeen
Three - Thalathh
Four – Arba'ah
Five - Khamsah
Six - Setah
Seven – Saba'ah
Eight - Thamaneah
Nine – Tesa'ah
Ten - Asharh
Eleven - Had a'ash
Twelve - Ithna'ash
Thirteen - Yhlata'ash
Fourteen - Arba'ata'ash
Fifteen- Khamista'ash
Sixteen- Sita'ash
Seventeen - Saba'ata'ash
Eighteen- Thamnta'ash
Nineteen – Tisataash
Twenty - Eshreen
Thirty – Thalatheen
Hundred – Meah
Thousand – Alf
Million - Malyon

CONCLUSION

Congratulations! You have completed all the tools needed to master the Arabic language, and I hope that this has been a valuable learning experience. Now you have sufficient communication skills to be confident enough to embark on a visit to Yemen, impress your friends, and boost your resume so good luck.

This program is available in other languages as well, and it is my fervent hope that my language learning programs will be used for good, enabling people from all corners of the globe and from all cultures and religions to be able to communicate harmoniously. After memorizing the required three hundred and fifty words, please perform a daily five-minute exercise by creating sentences in your head using these words. This simple exercise will help you grasp conversational communications even more effectively. Also, once you memorize the vocabulary on each page, follow it by using a notecard to cover the words you have just memorized and test yourself and follow that by going back and using this same notecard technique on the pages you studied during the previous days. This repetition technique will assist you in mastering these words in order to provide you with the tools to create your own sentences.

Every day, use this notecard technique on the words that you have just studied.

Everything in life has a catch. The catch here is just consistency. If you just open the book, and after the first few pages of studying the program, you put it down, then you will not gain anything. However, if you consistently dedicate a half hour daily to studying, as well as reviewing what you have learned from previous days, then you will quickly realize why this method is the most effective technique ever created to become conversational in a foreign language. My technique works! For anyone who doubts this technique, all I can say is that it has worked for me and hundreds of others.

NOTE FROM THE AUTHOR

Thank you for your interest in my work. I encourage you to share your overall experience of this book by posting a review. Your review can make a difference! Please feel free to describe how you benefited from my method or provide creative feedback on how I can improve this program. I am constantly seeking ways to enhance the quality of this product, based on personal testimonials and suggestions from individuals like you. In order to post a review, please check with the retailer of this book.

Thanks and best of luck,

Yatir Nitzany

Made in the USA
Las Vegas, NV
14 August 2023

76102261R00025